Life and Rhythms

LIFE AND RHYTHMS

A Collection of Poems By

IAN A. CAMPBELL

Adelaide Books
New York / Lisbon

2018

Life and Rhythms
A Collection of Poems
By Ian A. Campbell

Copyright © 2018 By Ian A. Campbell
Cover Image © 2018 A. F. Nikolic

Published by Adelaide Books, New York / Lisbon

Cover design & interior formatting:
Adelaide Books DBA, New York

Editor-in-Chief
Stevan V. Nikolic

All rights reserved. No part of this book may be reproduced in any manner whatsoever without written permission from the author except in the case of brief quotations embodied in critical articles and reviews.

For any information, please contact Adelaide Books
at info@adelaidebooks.org
or write to
Adelaide Books
244 Fifth Avenue, Suite D27
New York, NY, 10001

ISBN13: 978-1-949180-00-8
ISBN10: 1-949180-00-X

Printed in the United States of America

Dedicated

to Hyacinth, my flower that continues to bloom

&

Jarren, a son that continually shines.

Ian A. Campbell

Contents

Preface *11*

Rhythms in Choice

Windows *15*

Rightness *17*

What You Learn *18*

Confusion *19*

The Hunger *20*

Your Fight *21*

A Can *22*

Political Rhythms

The Right *25*

Mr. President *26*

A Man of Charm *27*

Successive *28*

Crowd Size *30*

Isolation *32*

Gods and Kings *33*

Rights and Rhythms

I Remember *37*

39 Violation
41 Individual Rights
43 Stolen Rights
46 Innate Right

Internal Rhythms

49 Company We Keep
50 The Fiend
51 Child in Wage
52 Pride
53 Internal Devil
54 Virtues
55 Nature
56 The Enlightened
57 Two Faces
58 Go Fish
59 The True Internal Self

Rhythms in Faith

63 By Fate
64 When Lost
66 Blind Faith
67 In Choice
68 In Sacrifice
70 Your Price

Rhythms of Hope

Joy   *73*

The Dark of Night   *74*

The Lonely   *75*

Depression   *76*

A Story   *78*

A Child   *79*

Rhythms of Love

Still Debating   *83*

Understandings   *84*

What's True   *85*

A Wish   *86*

Rhythms in Glory

Bonds   *89*

Glory   *90*

Courage   *92*

Childhood Dreams   *93*

Rhythms in the Past

What We Were   *97*

The Past   *98*

Regret   *99*

Island Breeze   *101*

Ships at Sea   *102*

103   The Pyramid

Rhythms in Truth

107   The Mask

108   Your Turn

109   Vice

110   The Mundane

111   The Lucky Few

112   In Dreams

113   In Greed

114   We Lie

115   Truth Depends

117   Right Expectations

Life and Rhythms

121   The City

122   The Monte

124   The Circus

125   The Unnecessary Walk

126   Your Dreams

128   Fiddler

Rhythms of Tomorrow

131   Time Is Limited

132   Time and Trade

134   In Age

Ian A. Campbell

The Curve   *135*
Times of Trouble   *137*
Clouds in Rainbow Skies   *138*
Today's Troubles   *139*
About the Author   *143*

Preface

Life and Rhythms is my second collections of poems. My first was *Life and Livity*, which started my explorations in societal truths. These poems represent my philosophical understanding of life and what's true in the human soul. I believe these poems are cathartic and seek to amplify the human spirit with an internal light. *Life and Rhythms* stands as my evolution as a poet, using strict meters, forms and rhyming schemes to put forth my philosophies. *Life and Rhythms* was brought about by long nights and a maddening passion to get each poem just right.

    The poems are our shared journeys, brimming with life lessons in a society in which we're increasingly lost. Life and Rhythms is a piece of work that demonstrates my growth and to this point it's the limit of my talents as a writer and a philosopher. I'm very proud of this book and truly believe it deserves to be shared now and for generations to come. Thank you for taking this journey with me.

Ian A. Campbell

Rhythms in Choice

LIFE AND RHYTHMS

Windows

What the eyes so behold, it's in mind we have preference.
As our reference frames all the seeds we're to sow,
It's our values that'll give all our deeds their significance.

But from windows, our values get blurred by rains.
As exposures reveal where our hearts got their stains,
It's our turmoil that signifies souls now carrying pains.

While at risk, we haven't eyes to negotiate fitness.
As those droplets obscure the most narrow of views,
It's the soul that must fight to become its own witness.

If the conscience refuses, our souls are then blind,
And behind those very windows, no values have claim.
We then hide, for we've chosen to live with no mind.

If we're blind, we depend on the kind for their eyes.
But, too, ghouls are then allowed to rule from on high.
For in choice, who can know what's in devil's own eyes?

If the shadows are perched on things that're unclear,
It's behind their very panes we retreat with our tears,
As those shysters abscond all that's moral by fear.

Ian A. Campbell

Should their negative reference create your preference,
Then the timely excuses that's used for circumstance,
Will not notice what's moral, for heavenly severance.

As no truth can be gained without our own eyes,
It's from panes you must challenge those perched on high.
In those windows they've framed, that anchors their lies.

Your acceptance without understanding is blindness,
So don't overlook the shadows your conscience can't place,
For the windows that're framed, invites all our madness.

What the eyes so behold, it's in mind we have preference.
And all timely excuses that's tied to our circumstance
Are the values we reference creating preference,
But for morals, its deeds that will hold our significance.

LIFE AND RHYTHMS

Rightness

When heart opposes actions, devils grin.
As doors are open tempting souls in sin,
It's only values held may claim your wins.

All things so won that hearts now claims in sin,
Will keep a devil warm who's eyeing storms;
For souls in guilt invite the devil's spin.

Where virtue's lost, its lies that claims those wins.
A mind in doubt, then funnel truth in tunnels,
Where souls, remain forever lost in winds.

In search of ease, your morals chasing breeze,
Now seeking gains by fate your heart's unclean,
And gains from lies can't justify those means.

As values void of work appears from stork.
Where goodness sought, no virtues ever so caught,
In choice, from thoughts to action, lies the fork.

On doors to rightness, truth will always knock,
The ones who answers, keep their souls intact.
If lies so win, the deaf so reap own sins;
As houses built so falls, the devil grins.

Ian A. Campbell

What You Learn

Where life is long, your soul must stay as strong.
What's known in youth, all fools regret in age,
And ripen fruits as sweet have seen some wrongs.

Those hiding truth won't grow to stage at age;
They'll leave what's true, no values souls can use,
As morals leaving, souls so turns the page.

Internal lies befall those shy, that said;
The lost then hides why; days now fly with lies,
As miseries found behind a life unlived.

In doubt, they oversteer curves that roads foretold.
Where goals got sold, they fishtail dreams of old,
Not taking lonely roads where values hold.

In goals, escapes we seek are laden traps,
A price so paid from choice, that takes a life,
Where beaten soul no longer see the gaps.

All things, once sure in youth, will change with age.
The wise must know at stage what wars they wage.
Whatever page you've caged, life's in phase,
So, turn the page, and seek your joy in days.

Confusion

They're spoken words without a meaning,
Those lost accepting lies that're based on feelings.
They're reeling, hating life while grieving
Can't find the ceiling, joy is leaving.

Where life's confusion holds illusions,
All treasures found can hold no pleasure;
Those looking blind won't see deceptions,
As meanings hold no truth to measure.

Refusing truth won't frame deficit,
If honesty inspects the ledger.
In loss or profit lives still commit,
So, yield to sense if truth's your measure.

Where honesty inspect the ledger,
Conclusions rest where values measured.
As truth must fight a mind that's clever,
The souls will pay for pulling lever.

If choice in mind does hold confusion
In lives compromised, truth is pliable.
When telling lies in self-deception,
As bell so tolls, whose soul is liable?

Ian A. Campbell

The Hunger

Innate, the hunger human soul so carries,
Our sins are tied to weights but never buried.
As souls so fight some lose the right, through worries.
Where water's deep, those lost will find what's horrid.

Innate, the hunger souls will always carry.
They're tied to weights as life reveals its worries.
Though hunger stems from wants our souls will marry,
They're tied to motives old, as days so hurries.

Innate the hunger; learnt the choice, we carry.
Where water's deep, our troubles bring the horrid.
Those sullied fight for gains without a worry,
And leave their victim's pains forever carried.

Where souls so fight the human hungers carried.
It's one's morality that tames the horrid.

LIFE AND RHYTHMS

Your Fight

Where things are true, the just must bear their fruits.
But know some currents fight a life that's true;
As souls that're tainted hinder just pursuits.

In life's pursuits, it's guilt the soul must atone,
A plight our souls so fight in right from light,
But choice announces builders casting stone.

As life will only greet what courage meets
Its roads, so laid where life shall know its path,
But souls will carry noise that darkness greets.

From darkness, life doesn't crest if mind's at rest.
Don't run without your sight to claim their works,
For sight and mind must face what life will test.

Don't fight a fight that's wrong, to name a plight,
If overgrown, not one's own, know you're alone,
And only declaration end those fights.

In fights that're true, the just must bear their fruits.
Where trees are hollow seeding wrong pursuits,
It's moving winds that'll fuel the cold's exposure,
And ones still fighting truth so finds no closure.

Ian A. Campbell

A Can

I saw a man with can in hand.
In crowd where found, on street I stand.
A can from hand,
A man with plan,
The can so lands, from man, from hand.

In dread and red, I nearly fled.
I bled from head and nothing said.
In right, I'll fight
In spite, I might
Just throw a stone to break his head.

Political Rhythms

The Right

When good doesn't draw its light from right,
At heaven's gate will evil so stand,
As devils demonstrate their might.

Where good doesn't fight, no choice is right;
The strong so hide internal light,
Not raising species near its height.

As devils demonstrate their might,
The weak on stage's concealing rage,
Where narrow minds encounter blight.

Without their means, the troupes will vote.
As right now turns from light to cope,
In guise, the worst now tweet their quotes.

As darkness chose to run from light,
The shadows cast their doubts on hope,
By leaving good no room to fight.

Where power stands as devils lore,
The heart unsure remains as poor.
As devils demonstrate their might,
The good must draw their light from right.

Ian A. Campbell

Mr. President

The first no worse than last, you've left no curse,
Your time now came and went, so please I'll vent.
The first to quench our thirst and dare the worst,
To raise their flags, to stand on morals bent.

A timid start, so legacy got caught.
In pride, with shoulders wide, your foes had room.
In power lust, they made their fuss from start.
As goons they swoon while taking out their brooms.

A legacy awry now under fist.
In truth, your ruling pen has laws at risk,
As worms in terms have surfaced, holding twists.
All claiming blind in race, but ghost in midst.

Where race's the silent fog that swirls in swamp,
The parties only vote on issues stamped.
Now changing winds have worms all glued in camps,
As devil's past so burns like wick from lamps.

The first, no curse and nowhere near the worst,
But hindsight, seeking right, must find the purse.
Your power stood reserved; a truth that preserves
An ideology no people deserve.

LIFE AND RHYTHMS

A Man of Charm

A man of charm who's warm, must weather storms
While staying calm whenever race so alarms.
With Michelle, living lean you hold your ohms,
While watching fiends with means so claim those calm.

With lines, you ran your electrifying currents
To breakers; modifying dreams once cursed.
Now boys and girls in house can pay their rents,
While seeking homes in pride to quench their thirst.

Your power covers vast reserves on towers,
That ran from lines now past augmenting hope.
You've shaken trees with roots of old that'll flower,
And circulate all kinds of weeds to cope.

You, man of charm has stayed calm through storms,
Our boys and girls now light their dreams with ohms.
The world's on alarm, as efforts gauge their surge,
Where houses old now buckle under purge.

Ian A. Campbell

Successive

In your great coronation,
From the heights in ascension
Could you give us a mention?

As my interest is porous,
The intention is ever us.
There's no need for the chorus.

But because it's your stew;
You could give us a clue
Of an eagle in view.

In my "view," not aggressive.
You'll be judged as passive
Yet you've won in successive.

In us, hope still so rages.
You're a case for the ages,
As your time's now in pages.

But in peace, you've no prize.
For in wars, there were cries.
Too many died, more in lies.

LIFE AND RHYTHMS

If in hope, you're still wise.
Where's your mention of dogs,
Now in heat for your prize.

For your names' own ascension,
It's your time for a mention,
Just forget there's a pension,
And just give us a mention.

Ian A. Campbell

Crowd Size

The untruths are his highs.
If the crowd will not rise,
He'll continue his lies.

Where did rectitude lose?
Yes, an actor we choose,
So, the lies shouldn't so bruise.

As he watches the size,
It so compromises the prize,
While still trying the wise.

As he speaks, what so flies?
As I listen, it's noise,
With no answers to cries.

It's in hate he so waits,
His supporters are late
And their souls on the make.

They can't see where's the right,
As they've caged the light,
That once loomed very bright,

LIFE AND RHYTHMS

To the red, let them rue,
As we leave those in blue
And so search all that's true.

If the facts are our highs;
We the people must rise
And so stop all those lies.

Ian A. Campbell

Isolation

Where brotherhood so searches thrills,
In hills, by grills, as bonds so builds,
A mind's isolation finds what fills.

In bars, as talk will light cigars,
To battles lost from roguish wars.
A mind's isolation loses scars.

In country clubs, where dollars rub,
And names on plates will try to snub.
A mind's isolation finds its club.

In arenas loud, where owner owns,
And uses talents time bemoans.
A mind's isolation makes no loans.

The border wars on stage from rage,
Are against those caught just looking wage.
Yet mind's isolation hold its cage.

When souls aren't filled, hearts don't build,
But mind's isolation fit those bills;
The lost forget all life's a thrill
And only trade can build our hills.

LIFE AND RHYTHMS

Gods and Kings

Authorities and laws required start,
So gods and kings thus cast the rules that last.
From wreckage, captive minds now lost are caught,
But days will find their truth in future's past.

Still tribal, minds must fight untended soul.
By right we move from old as books foretold.
The mind must fight to shed what's dead and cold,
Or souls will cling to dying thoughts of old.

On roads still dark from past in days of might,
Where David took Goliath's sight by right.
He fought the plagues then stealing souls by fright.
And left us choice to claim in minds our plight.

Our fear of lost begins from mind's own springs,
As doubt so swims we've lost in life our hymns.
Where gods and kings are merely mind's own sling,
Supporting hollow souls on broken limbs.

The passing drums of time resounds by chorus,
Where fading noise are shielding fields of locusts.
As swarm envelopes kings to times own purpose,
The gods still feed in fear and steer those nervous.

Ian A. Campbell

As rule of law no longer needs a start,
The future wreckage lies where gods are caught;
Where caged rabid beasts now fat from feast,
Have left their troubles great in minds they've fleeced.

Rights in Rhythms

I Remember

In thoughts, on rolling greens,
With Robin's breast in autumn's best,
Recalling hate in scenes.

It's thirteen, I remember,
Where fears, and doubts, infected
A mind still young and tender.

On scenic trails as partners,
With shield on chest in autumn,
Where wolves who sprung from corners.

Up-close I met the venal.
My heart they tore apart,
As brutes are always penal.

In fist were batons, firm, and
With grip, they hit; I slipped,
Midsection, blows still landed.

As lynching past their craving,
My shackles trigger images
Of darken fruits still hanging.

Ian A. Campbell

My grace then hid my place,
As soul now breaks, I realized
Their hate was mine to face.

A truth my heart now states;
Though spirit's sometimes late,
The years have healed faith.

A mind once young and tender,
Refusing hate remembers,
By plan, or coincidence,
All lives afford incidents.

LIFE AND RHYTHMS

Violation

Whether day or night, I'll fight.
I'm a witness…truth must stand.
Right by God, by sight, I might
Take a life from land by hand.

Heavy the heart demanding fight,
Heavy my soul still wanting right.
Right by God, in sight; still might
Take a life from God by right.

I'm a witness…soul must stand
Hiding truth may hurt my plans.
Scars from seeing blows that land.
Heart now carries shame in hands.

I'm a witness…fights in night,
Hearing mother's cries till light;
Hurts a heart in part from fright,
Killing soul's own will to fight.

I'm a witness…mother's shame,
Morning blame no villains claimed.
Hope and pride still never waned,
Nursing pain as tears so rained.

Ian A. Campbell

Whether day or night, I'm sure,
Violets bloom with darken moons.
Sores of old, will make the score,
Leaving scabs that looms from goon.

Life's my witness…truth will stand,
Stand by right in God's own hands.

Individual Rights

A quest that only life can choose.
A right forever set in time.
A gift that only minds can praise.
A truth that justice owes to thine.

Where rights tomorrow needed start,
It's only minds can hold its flame.
As pages turn all lives are caught,
But each must take their rights by claim.

In liberty a nation loss,
As founding fathers set to task.
From birth a nation bearing cross,
With slaves in hand they're wearing masks.

While leaving ages dark they stood
With plans in hands on stolen lands;
On parchment, rights were signed in blood,
As seeds of justice sown in plans.

The right to choose that souls so pursues,
Are destinations holding truths.
As death's the cue to life's own clues,
It's goals that bear the ripest fruits.

Ian A. Campbell

A quest that only values choose.
A right forever owed thine,
Are seeds that only souls can raise,
By deeds from trees that grow in time.

From ages dark tomorrow's task
Must pay the bill all rights so ask.
The right to mind's own property
Is one's own right in clarity!

LIFE AND RHYTHMS

Stolen Rights

Where liberty so stands, who'll claims the human plight?
If force's the only wrong, what nation state has light?
As time's the only fight, what goals in life are right?

The burial grounds to pass will leave their storied choice,
Where time's the test we've found in suffrage Marxist graves,
Depraved fascist souls still holding human's vice.

While seeming fair, is democracy the only good?
When great majorities have claimed choice by right,
And skews the mind's own choice by knife in history's blood.

When rights in count have justified a greater good.
Its liberty they steal while sounding number's count.
The troupes in count deny what's true and dawn their hoods.

Where stolen rights are justified by greater good,
The mobs forget the smallest right belongs to one;
With vote they steal your claim to choice, as mobs would.

In numbers, shoulders lighten weights that one should bear.
In fear we turn to mobs and hope they're just in votes,
Forgetting mind's own right to hope and cope in fear.

Ian A. Campbell

In fear the mobs now hold the keys where souls are poor.
They sling their mud and chew their cud while choking rights,
We fail by splitting fights for rights, forgetting chore.

In liberty what's right, if mobs have made their heist,
With laws that hijack choice to name another's good.
Without your choice it's liberty that pays the price.

Where civil rights' the fight, who writes the rules on field,
When bets are set, who vets where limitations met,
As lives corrupted steals our meal to seal the deal.

As rights when lacking justice even no playing field.
Assenting action wins no lasting right, a station;
But quest for rights may steal a truth while donning shield.

All rights we separate in turn then violate,
As facts now move from grounds as found to find their shade.
It's stolen rights, now justified, that take the bait.

Where liberty doth stand, all's equal in minds' pursuits,
Yet having rights can't shatter mind's own ceiling;
For fishes lost remain the bait to win recruits.

In life the liberty to pursue holds our grounded stick,
As mind's own right to property so elevates
The distance reached, laws that're false have sorted tricks.

LIFE AND RHYTHMS

As liberty must stand, who'll claims the human plight?
As force's the only wrong, what nation state has light?
As time's the only fight, what goals in life are right?
As being bears the only choice, what's right in fight?

Ian A. Campbell

Innate Right

No action holds a path innately right.
No journey finds inaction making fight.
But driven lives are bent on proving;
Between the two it's pride that's choosing.

Inaction loses fights by right in night.
Where life's your muse, it's day we claim by right.
For sake of night, a life in pride is woven;
For lack of faith, a life remains unproven.

When time becomes the beast you fear in cage,
Remember, lives onstage have fights to wage.
Though life may twist, don't ever you miss a tryst.
From mist, a heart must find a life in bliss.

Where courage meets your action, life's a fight,
But fear's inaction holds no path that's right.

Internal Rhythms

Company We Keep

The company we keep
Are often ones we seek;
What's found, our virtues reap.

Decisions scatter seeds
As judgment takes the lead,
But choice must pull the weeds.

The kind will whine if blind,
So devils' shelters lie,
To hide what truth may find.

As water settles ground,
The pond may hold the stone,
Where honesty is found.

If soul can't find what seed,
You'll find the signs of greed,
A truth we seldom need.

As devils' words are kind,
It's deeds that'll show their signs.
Where judgment takes the lead,
You'll watch all devils plead.

Ian A. Campbell

The Fiend

If hearts unclean, no ends defend their means,
But actions tells a truth that soul so feel;
With lustful hearts, it's green that plays the fiend.

As fiends pretend on ends where friends so stands
They don their shields in means as hearts unseen.
The fiends then turns from heart to claim in hands.

Where hearts unclean and minds unseen in means,
They'll look for mules as tools to rule as fools,
Without a mind they'll hold all lines in scenes.

Still fiends will stand in fanes and cast their blame.
With souls that're lost refusing God's own shame,
No guilt as brutes' recruits, in search of fame.

No dog salute by name, so watch the claim.
Your life's a fight, though slight still claim its heights;
But watch the fiends in fane who seek to maim.

When hearts unclean and minds unseen in means,
The fiends at times will shift their shape in scenes.
As winds so blow, it's time that places foes.
If eyes so knows, remove your heart from crows.

LIFE AND RHYTHMS

Child in Wage

If you're playing a part, don't get caught in what's sought;
Where a child, not in age but in wage, is on stage.
That very actor, has methods while playing a part.

As the hunter now feasts, it's the tame that's the game.
It's your flames that die in their reign, and that's plain.
They divert as they claim you in worth, while they blame.

When a child who's in wage, yet not age, is on stage,
Don't accept degradation and hope it's a phase.
For in cage, there's no place to escape those in rage.

If you're playing a part, you'll get caught in what's sought.
In what's found, where the crowd is too loud, don't be proud,
For no crowd has the price of your heart when it's caught.

If you take them on flings, in their spins are their sins.
They may hide in the spotlight, to blind all their blight.
So before you so pledge, it's to know what you'll win.

If you're playing a part, don't get caught in what's sought.
Where there's method, the actor's too, playing a part.
If so caught, understanding the art is your start,
To remove what's in heart from untrustworthy farts.

Ian A. Campbell

Pride

In vanity, we're caught, and I too, sip from cup.
Arrive in need, yet seeking comforts tied to wants;
We're mixed up and wanting life all fixed up;
Not realizing battles fought in pride don't haunt.

For values, fights are fought; if false, it's pride that walks.
On streets with mirrors, eyes reflect where sorrows hide.
Those living false will try to guise a life with talk,
While leaving soul's reflection holding hopes that've died.

In stares, all eyes reflecting fears are one's own nightmares,
Those eyes then cultivate those seeds that're blooming weeds.
As false reflections run with times, unfounded fears,
No mirrors holding cracks can sprout what's good from seeds.

All vanity is false, the souls that're wearing masks,
Have long been cast from images vast in one's own past.
Yet, pride hasn't time to waste when truth in self isn't asked.

Internal Devil

In greed, there's dream, we ought not dream,
The dark of night may stir what heart
So hides and go to fish from stream.

If flames in values burn as someday,
The scriptures hold no light in night,
As inner devil's out to play.

At dawn, you'll bargain night with right.
As morning's haze, forget the blaze;
Where right got lost in glare of night.

When wishes fish without any rules.
The pilot's lit with minds unfit,
As wishes bore unwanted mules.

Where conscience fears no heaven's light,
The devil's heart may stay to play,
While twisting night and stealing right.

The dreams we dream, we ought not dream.
May seem too real, when loin's in steam.
If night so plucks the right from stream,
It's values held that protects team.

Ian A. Campbell

Virtues

From morals, virtues tell what's true in self.
The self-that's spotted true, by ones insightful.
The self-that's envied close, by ones on shelves.
The self-that's feared wide, by ones still fearful.

It's time that plays the cards that life has dealt.
And virtues reap all truth that lies in self.
As troubles fleece those virtues souls once meant;
Our souls will bear the cost of dreams on shelves.

Where truth still seeps in dreams, desires still lives.
No lie can hide internal gifts so felt,
But gifts aren't tied to one's perspectives;
They're tied to honesty so felt and kept.

Where dreams are lost, don't ever you live reactive,
For joys are reaped by hands and minds still active.
No gifts are ever as lost if mind's proactive,
But pride must run from lives that're lived collective.

From morals, virtues held are truths in self,
And virtues lost will steal a soul's own health.
In time, all play the cards that life has dealt,
But hold what's true in self as souls was meant.

LIFE AND RHYTHMS

Nature

It's choice that tells your nature,
But nature bends to process,
As action finds where's pressure.

Where pressure wills character,
Its virtues held we measure,
Without we watch those clever.

The actor acts, remember,
And players play with values,
As fans, so sit in slumber.

Where clues do curse the clueless,
Remember life's a scramble,
And only action's boundless.

In work, its pride we measure;
No one can steal your labor,
But choice will find where's pleasure.

If hope invites your pleasure,
As vice so haunts your nature;
Its choice that'll find where's pressure,
As truth so takes the measure.

Ian A. Campbell

The Enlightened

A mind in quest for wisdom stays as blind.
As knowledge holds no end to minds in search,
All steps from thoughts will leave the blind behind.

A life unaware shouldn't last, so leave as past.
Where goals exceed our boundaries, bets are set,
And cards where knowledge cast, tomorrow's vast.

We fight our past to claim a better day.
The one's enlightened never wait on night
To make their claim, as night will carry ways.

As time's the stage, what's cast by type won't last.
In days all rage will change for life's in phase,
So live beyond the past, where die's now cast.

No mind in quest of knowledge stays as blind,
And minds without any boundaries, wisdom finds.

LIFE AND RHYTHMS

Two Faces

One exists as two; just watch the signs—
One that's seen, aspired, one that's reached.
Only toil can find what talent hides.
Truth in self survives where troubles breach.

Lies in self betray your currency,
Lies so told will roll on roads unpaved,
Leaving minds committing truancy;
Hiding one's own lies where souls have caved.

Larceny begins on creaking floors,
Windows open, doors to souls unsure.
Minds secure protect the souls that're poor,
Leaving thieves what fools have left by doors.

One exists as two; don't fight the signs;
Only toil reveals what inside hides.

Ian A. Campbell

Go Fish

In waters vast our efforts fish.
Where currents' strong who'll get ensnared?
Where tortoise fish and hares so wish,
Whose net when cast will bring what's earned.

Tomorrow's truths all lives must bear.
It's fear and doubt the tortoise wears,
While hares are quick for lives in glare;
Yet none escapes the thing that snares?

As time the snare no matter pair,
In waters vast all kinds must fish.
As only fight escapes its glare,
It's net so cast, so makes the dish.

All life's in chance, so make effort
Your spear where fears and doubts are clear.
The wise so knows, no life has worth,
Where souls decline to fight its fears.

In waters vast all lives must fish,
The nets we cast is one's own share.
No hare can fish from tortoise's dish,
So tortoise, never mind that hare.

LIFE AND RHYTHMS

The True Internal Self

The true internal self is always felt,
The truth behind your wine, their lime, those kind,
Can't help a life when false aesthetics melt.

A life that's true will always stem from root.
As forest covers hedge; we see no shoots,
Whereby we leave the self still hiding loot.

A mind in haze forgets to pull the weeds
Until they're trees where dreams no longer seeds.
As dreams get bent, they help no fallen trees.

In weeds, the inner self will fight what's felt.
As pricks from thorns now pierce the heart with fear,
It's time that'll cloud the mind from grounds, unkept.

In battles loss, the soul then plays the host,
The worst so lies and alters life's own course,
As houses harbor self-invited ghosts.

The true internal self is always felt,
Behind all things that're false, aesthetics melt.
When failures judged shows the soul what's clear,
Those honest find in truth all flaws that're near.

Rhythms in Faith

LIFE AND RHYTHMS

By Fate

Awaiting fate can help no one be great,
All stolen plate in time the truth shall state;
Without your faith tomorrow's life you'll hate.

Unearned greatness creates one's own bait
Desiring status, wishing treasures, souls
So hide its reason's treason, tempting fate.

But wait, all suicides make unclear a reason,
No note attests the souls' betrayal in faith,
That point where rhyme and reason made their treason.

The young in mind will live for gangster's ruse,
If treason holds a reason, values chose,
A truth that takes a time before a bruise.

No hunter knowing seasons eats by fate,
As bears won't wait to eat then hibernate.
If late, who knows whose fate may rest on plate?

Awaiting fate won't help create what's great.
If action's late, tomorrow hide fate.
For sure, the lost don't see the meat on plate,
By fate, they wait, while losing lives once great.

Ian A. Campbell

When Lost

In rain, we seek a life mundane.
Where souls retreat and lies repeat,
To follow steps, bechance insane.

Where truth is lost, some find the cross;
Some fast, some go to mass, while cursing,
What rass! Pretending noble class.

Internal silence bears the cross.
Awaiting thunder, finds those lost.
At heaven's gates, we'll see the cost.

All lives untrue so finds the gray,
Forgetting days when children played
And looking ways the righteous prays.

As lies subvert the mind in faith,
Those lost now claiming higher state,
Forgetting one's own plight awaits.

Where ends don't mend their times are slight,
They'll wait at stations, seeking light,
As souls forget the joys from fight.

LIFE AND RHYTHMS

As train's now late the pains ingrain,
So souls retreat and days repeat,
To follow ways, bechance insane.

Those wearing masks, their souls are lost,
Their lives can't atone what sins now cost.
As truth is lost, some'll find the cross,
Some'll fast, some'll go to mass, what rass!

Ian A. Campbell

Blind Faith

Where life so throws its blows, your faith's the foe?
If faith is late, reality ain't straight,
And shaken faith won't help a life with woes.

In woes, as spirit's low, you watch for crows.
In troubles, vultures stay in sight to smite;
They cover grounds as faith now hide in holes.

In faith, where minds are blind, perspective's late.
Don't cope with hope if mind can't find the ropes,
As blows will choke all hope in drunken state.

A life in shaken faith can't help with woes.
No one can know your faith no matter state,
But know your wins will stand to silence foes.

Tomorrow's sorrows hold their place; don't chase.
The race is yours to face, so find its pace.
It's will that fills the gaps that faith can't place.

When lost, if minds are blind, perspective's late;
And fears that emanate confirms no faith.
As shaken faith can't help a life with woes,
It's courage fighting doubts that'll stops your foes.

In Choice

Our greatest choice is made by fate,
Succeeding choices make those great.
In choice, it's hard to keep all straight,
Yet courage rests on offered plate.

On rocks, foundations strong are laid.
In choices weighed, knowledge stays.
If effort's true, your time has grade
But hope in days will carry ways.

Conditions stand before any choice,
Yet action makes all lives unsure.
Position pays a higher price,
If minds already claim a score.

Tomorrow's scores are never sure,
It's choices made that'll tell the score.

Ian A. Campbell

In Sacrifice

The spirit alone so knows it's sacrifice,
As eyes can only see a moral choice,
The soul is left now holding virtues' price.
But bleeding hearts will know their virtues vice.

Whenever quenching thirst, your throat is first,
Your belly's never worst when throat is nursed.
The self is first and whether liked, cursed,
The soul shouldn't claim the worst from other's purse.

Where ones are selfless, sacrifices creep.
They're meek, it's air most rarified seek.
They're trading needs, while letting others reap.
Can't reach a moral peak as virtues weak.

The spirit alone so knows it's sacrifice,
As eyes can only see a moral choice.
Your bleeding heart will know your virtues vice,
While leaving souls in shame with moral's price.

Where sacrifice's your pill, your virtue's lost.
It's pride you swallow, holding virtues' mask.
The self is first; all souls must bear those cost,
You'll see the ask when virtues set to task.

If false, morality so holds the knife;
Your choice is only made as eyes have framed heist.
The choice then hold your souls internal strife,
Accepting claims where virtues holds no choice.

As true morality is never wrong,
It's only values held can change its stance.
All values lost to morals find those strong,
As virtues reap its name to soul's expanse.

Remember, hearts so know your sacrifice,
But eyes can only see the moral choice;
Yet hearts must come to know their virtues vice,
For soul will always pay the price of choice.

Ian A. Campbell

Your Price

Where things derive by lies, there's cost so tied,
A price the conscience charges souls inside.
As values lose their worth, the spirit hides;
The blame arrives, as souls now want off ride.

The damage conscience charges souls inside,
Reflects morality of one's not trying;
They're pitching crowds that're loud, and seeking buy-in;
A losing fight that'll leave a soul, still dying.

As values lose their worth, and souls so hide,
Corrupted souls by choice won't see the heist.
You'll thrive in spite, but life demands its price.
A price, that'll claim their worth in pride or vice.

As blame arrives, the soul will take the ride,
But after facing shame, they'll know the price.
Where souls aren't equipped, pride is lost in heist—
A fact our soul's own shame must face from choice.

When things derive by lies, a cost's so tied,
As values lose their worth, whose soul now dies?

Rhythms of Hope

Joy

In joy we float on wings as spirit sings.
It's life's internal grin that claims our wins.
But joy can't stays when tied to passing flings.
So firm your grip and look beyond those sins.

As souls with compromised ellipse may flip,
You'll find your balance putting weights on hips.
When stories flip, your courage writes the script,
But know no lasting joys can come from whips.

As joys so float on wings, we manage winds.
In life's commotion faith cajoles emotions,
The clouds we meet are merely one's chagrin,
In life's unending search for one's elation.

The brilliant vapor holding moments true
Are life's own nimbus washing away blues.
They're wedded deeds from clouds of fears and flings,
Where joys now floats on wings as souls so sings.

Ian A. Campbell

The Dark of Night

Your lonely soul so cries in dark of night,
Here under moon while fearing tides in room;
Are pharaohs sizing tombs, awaiting lights
Of Ra, as winds of Amun so spell their doom.

In dread of night the mind so loses fights,
As doors are open to torments, holding judgment.
Where souls now feel the bitter cold of night,
The sadness felt invites all devils sent.

Your heart now beats with fear to souls' despair,
As nothing's clear, you're watching ghouls appear.
Where winds of Amun disrupt your soul with fear,
In pillows drenched, heart so sheds its tears.

All souls now sizing tombs, but seeking light;
Must turn to see our moon's majestic sight.

LIFE AND RHYTHMS

The Lonely

The lonely wear a mask that troubles cast.
In night, we're easily lost behind what's masked.
At dawn we drown our sorrows deep in flask,
So foggy haze can hide what's foul when asked.

In rooms once bid secure, we find suffrage,
Where self-imposed darkness holds what bothers.
As minds now lose their place to give refuge
Ours joys tomorrow hinge on winds from others.

When doubts are casting lines in muddy waters,
You cope, or soul begins its downward slope.
If ripples spread invading silent rivers;
The laden curls as vines surrounding hope.

To find tomorrow's truths, we look to faith,
Where lonely roads we face are stolen grace.
No matter state, there's life from troubles great,
Your limitation lies in time and space.

We're meant to wear our mask from troubles past
It's strength our troubled past should cast, if asked.
So find a life of pride behind what's masked,
And let no troubles hinder one's own task.

Ian A. Campbell

Depression

Where time's unused, darkest caves are open,
As hidden devils spring from dark, awoken;
They carry buried pains from wounds, unspoken.

It starts where warm; the soul doesn't hear the alarm.
As life's dependent fragilities now dawn,
A mind not knowing worth can find no calm.

As feelers mount, invading silent rivers,
The mermaid surfaces, stirring muddy waters.
She hides her tail with scales, as water shimmers.

Her sirens beckon pains that burn in veins.
Her tempting trance, our lost romance in glance,
Now leaves the water's edge exposing pains.

As souls' dependent fragilities so dawns.
Our mind's internal lies can soothe no cries,
For trouble's full on, facing life's own scorn.

You stand, alone in crowds, as thoughts retreat,
Your jealous beauty longs for lonely nights,
Where lies repeat, so eyes no longer greet.

LIFE AND RHYTHMS

Support in truth can bring no remedy,
For truths are tied to lies; as souls so hide,
Morbidity now haunts your melody.

The soul must be awoken, hope is choking,
No longer coping, devil's stealing tokens.
The mind must look around for doors that're open
And try to heal those wounds with words that're spoken.

Ian A. Campbell

A Story

A life that's young in history fights for glory.
From growing pains, all souls must tell their story.
As time's our bondage, lives must claim their dowry.

As ticking clocks so span our years by days,
The gift of thought, our moral ought from start,
Must know the heart's own maze will carry ways.

As life so follows time, we'll find some grieving.
Before the cycles make their rounds to ground,
The truth that's found must know all souls are leaving.

The souls that're lost will find their truth in mourning,
They're hoping ways in days reveals their maze,
But seeking right in evening, claiming meaning.

Tomorrow whips all tears, so never fear.
If losses stain, no tears may wash as clean;
They're moments caught, that begs a hearts to share.

A life that's young in history fights for glory.
From growing pains, all souls must tell a story.
At journey's end, remember, life is glory.
Wherever night does fall, what tells your story?

LIFE AND RHYTHMS

A Child

There're things a child so learns unspoken.
In ways of lies, their minds aren't broken.
Where lies are spoken, hearts are stolen
And only time can tell what's taken.

There're things a child so learns unspoken.
No hard realities, yet broken.
As truth in words are simply taken,
Your lies in love will leave them open.

There're things a child so learns unspoken.
In love without your terms, they're broken.
Accepting tokens tied to spoken,
And hoping speaker's mind isn't broken.

There're things a child so learns that're spoken.
In ways of truth, their hearts are open.
From words their pride's too often taken,
Where joys of life unproven, stolen.

There're things a child so learns unspoken.
Whatever hardships times has woven,
Though choking, choose your words while coping;
And find all ways their hearts are breaking.

There're things a child will learn unspoken,
So tend their lives before they're broken.

Rhythms of Love

LIFE AND RHYTHMS

Still Debating

In shallow waters, flings I find…
So strong I hold to rein in sin.
Of strings in water, fears are mine.

Debating life, awaiting song,
In note, I hope its lines I wrote,
So life and rhythms, may stay as strong.

As fading picture lies in glance,
The fool in comfort lives no life,
Awaiting song, debating chance.

Where ponds are still, our time's the fight,
It's knowing light from days is night,
As currents keep a life not right.

The fear of sharing keeps me warm,
A fool remaining calm in storm;
Still watching winds of time, unalarmed.

In storm, still swimming shallow ponds
Where flawless love invites the cons.
My fear of loss prevents my gain,
Not knowing greed has left its stain.

Ian A. Campbell

Understandings

In the past, I was lost, for we moved too fast.
It was days, us in steam, when my heart had to scream;
Understandings got lost at some points in our past.

In the bush, I so looked, with bird still in hand.
Now my bird, in her right, not my sight, was in flight,
A reality leaving me nothing in hand.

To my luck, at the table, her feelings still able.
I'm now stable and willing to make this our ride.
It's with pride; it's no lie as I fight for the fable.

In the past, we were lost, as we moved too fast.
If tomorrow is going to last, it's in task,
But today we must look what's beyond that that's past.

When we fight, will you promise to meet me with care?
In my wrongs, when offended, be kind and so teach,
And in time, we'll deserve all that life has to share.

On those days, don't you fear; our tomorrow is cast.
We'll forgive that which passed when moved too fast.
If tomorrow is going to last, it's in task,
But today, we must move from beyond what has passed.

What's True

As love rewards those holding strong to truth.
Those holding lies recite in name those great;
Not knowing loves that's true are tended fruits,
And seeds that're lost are lies beset by fate.

Where love won't break a dollar looking cents,
It's faith in love that climbs those costly hills;
A price, when paid, so worth all love's expense,
Unpaid, a cost in years as love so spills.

When false, it's love that fails to hear the truth;
You hide with lies as lovers' claims deride.
In love, we live with lies when truth is moot,
So challenge brutes, where lies in love may hide.

Where love rewards those holding strong to truth,
It's love that stems from years of tended roots.

Ian A. Campbell

A Wish

My heart got lost behind familial masks,
Our love's in stress, bechance familial wants.
We're caught, from love that steals ancestral tasks,
As I the heretic, the devil taunts.

Where love must fight, in days our love may stray.
Absurdities then look to steal what's real.
As guiltless love now fights where night has play.
With pain, their shadows haunt a love that feels.

All love requires the bold if gates to hold.
In dueling faiths, the fight's too great to wait.
Traditions ambush thoughts we never scold,
As flames now die in night from devils great.

If love is taut and families still haunts,
Be mindful, love is fighting devil's taunts.

Rhythms in Glory

Bonds

The bonds of wars are far till lives at risk,
In frantic hours the primal soul's in midst,
Where even the doves shall stand to make a fist.

In stories told, that's never held but sold.
The primal molds the cultivated soul,
Where truth disrupts all faiths in stories old.

Where brotherhood so builds against their mortar,
In frantic hours, their oaths can see no sins
As soldiers bond, like cedar swells to water.

Where souls do hold to life a little longer,
It's fear that creates human bonds with strangers,
As love of brothers, creates souls that're stronger.

In wars, they'll toil for survival from rivals.
As frantic hours now put their truths at risk,
It's hearts that're primal stirs their soul's revival.

As soldiers fight with guns against all mortars,
All soldiers' bonds like cedar swells to water;
For under duress promises made are stronger,
As souls so hold to life a little longer.

Ian A. Campbell

Glory

They're born to blaze a life of glory.
Among the stars, while having scars, they're bound,
Unbought, their loyalty so tells their story.

The young who're looking ways in days will sign.
To end with bends, they'll find said friends who mend.
In time that's lent, I hope their days are kind.

The young now finding ways in days have signed.
In time, their hearts become unclean by fiends,
As storms in deserts turn their conscience blind.

Those trying, crying—friends are dying, signed!
To whom it's done…it's war; in lives, it's scars.
As deaths so finds no reason, lives are marred.

Those lost in killing fields will know no peace,
Because beliefs no longer rest at feet.
There're coming nights when quiet noise won't cease.

As conscience peers in fear to one's own nightmares.
The soul must justify all deeds unclear;
Where palsy's hiding truth that souls can't share.

The young once looking ways in days did sign,
But found all bends, no ends, while losing friends.
The time so lent to thine, they found unkind.

In wars, it's lords that'll steal their lives, remember;
As May, November, claims as one all members.
It's love and loyalty that'll tell the story,
Of heroes surviving hell to find no glory.

Ian A. Campbell

Courage

As fear is never planned,
Who knows where courage stands?
Those strong will find in hand.

You're born to know some sadness,
But leave it up to courage
To find where life has kindness.

In gains your will is tested,
And troubles check a life
To see if truly vested.

Don't hide in fear and wait;
You're born to know the fight,
But nerves don't stand innate.

Your courage's never late,
And primacy won't flake,
If kept atop the plate.

As devils seek the meek,
Your courage wakes those weak.
The strong will find in hand.
If only heart would stand.

LIFE AND RHYTHMS

Childhood Dreams

Those grieving dreams as time's still moving,
Are out of place as caricatures
In thoughts unseen but always looming.

If childhood dreams remain unframed,
It's only work that'll anchor journeys,
As days await all names so claimed.

Those lost will walk in fields of imaginings,
Desiring dreams no longer present;
As hollow souls, now sway by inklings.

Where lies so meet reality,
Fulfillment runs to distant places,
Revealing destination's frailty.

As goals unreached find what's scary,
It's middle age that'll hold our query,
If deeds haven't reaped lives of glory.

All destinations live with frailties;
Your hearts must face realities.
Where life will end, there's one that's pictured.
Where life is lived, one's so captured.

Rhythms in the Past

LIFE AND RHYTHMS

What We Were

We are what we were,
While being who we are.
So far, we've waged wars,
Trying to be stars.

Yet it's from our scars,
We pick out life shards
And be who we are
From that which we were.

In pain all so sails,
The lost ships will wail,
As bright stars too fall
In life's timely call.

We are what we were,
And that which we are
Cannot be undone.
It's time in the sun
That may yet transform
All our lives past storms.

Ian A. Campbell

The Past

In the race we so face, it's those rabbits
For the course that're unseating our habits.

As our past will remain ours to face;
All that's buried will carry its trace.

It's with context; we slow it in place.
To the turtle, who's keeping your pace?

As our feelings can sometimes be blind;
It's from sight where the mind must so dine.

But all feasts have their limits till passed;
So when looking too long, who's the ass?

When the mind can't discern where's the wrong,
It's in hope; it affects those once strong.

From the past it's self-blame that has stains,
If the soul now can't heal its own pains.

In the race we so face, it's those rabbits
For the course that unseat all our habits.

So the turtles must know how to step,
And too, also remember missteps.

Regret

You cannot know what's sadness
Until you know regret.
You cannot know what's madness
Until you've made that bet.

You cannot win that bet
Until you've made the climb.
You cannot know regret
Until you're given time.

The blessed find regret,
When looking back too long.
Until tables are set,
Regret affects those strong.

You cannot know regret
Until you've met with failure.
Where minds aren't always set,
Whose judgment claims your future?

No one can find their courage,
Until their will decides.
When pride so turns the page,
You gauge the ride; don't glide.

Ian A. Campbell

As shame can't anchor pride,
No lie can overcome failure.
When soul reveal what hides
It's one own heart we measure.

LIFE AND RHYTHMS

Island Breeze

I remember swaying trees while feeling breeze;
On veranda, mind so ganders; soul's in wonder.
Days from stolen dreams, as paint and brush so found these,
Smiles with glee; it's I who's pleased; life's my wonder.

I was raised in Friendship; our land so worshiped.
Boys and girls by ponds in twirl, as feelings swirl.
Boots and bell-bottoms were hip, not pleased when ripped.
Flying kites till night, no lights, as minds unfurl.

Lions so hide their courage; ghosts now play the host.
Faith's delusions turn unclean by hands unseen.
Voodoo changes future's past and works at cost.
Time has passed; things got lost without their means.

I remember island breeze in trees, so pleased.
Days of dreams, were scenes from paint and brush, indeed.

Ian A. Campbell

Ships at Sea

In storms, some ships remain at sea.
They're set adrift by winds from ghosts;
With damaged hulls, they try to be.

In time, as drama comes, they're caught.
A soul in want, its kindness sought,
As trauma hides tomorrow's fraught.

Where damage sets your mind on course,
You're cast adrift while fighting ghosts;
Connections, broken, hide the source.

To leave your past, put down the mask;
No one can thrive in noise when guised
As days, so listen; life will ask.

A mind that's under strain can wane;
You'll fight in vain, carrying pain,
As villains make no claims in rain.

In storms, some ships remain at sea;
With damaged hulls, they try to be.
While seeking port, your damaged past
Must lose the mask if hopes to last.

LIFE AND RHYTHMS

The Pyramid

As whippings course the stones, whose blood to ground?
When spirit's broken, faith will turn on truth;
As time so moves, the stones become what's found.

In violation, rights by man so reigned.
In times now past, they've built entombed fanes.
In violation, rights by birth they've claimed.

In bloodlines, only thought decided crimes.
As thieves, they hid the freedoms life designed,
While victims lived poverty of times.

From Egypt to Spain, they maim; all souls they claim.
With stone, they've broken backs with wooden axe,
While human cost so taxes heaven's shame.

We gain in shame if truth forgets there's blame.
In times now past, truths bearing cross are lost,
As stories told, though foul, all spirits claim.

Today in shrines by mass those lost arrive
In pride, forgetting slants to breath of sight.
On grounds, though beauties found, still look around;
Some apex steals a past where suffrage found.

Rhythms in Truth

LIFE AND RHYTHMS

The Mask

I see the pride that hides behind your eyes,
Your broken heart has left a life once proud.
The mask you wear from fear, too, tells the why.
As gaze, so whispers troubles heard as loud.

Where minds so move with crowds, your soul has blame.
In mass, they come and go; just watch their flow.
In trains, in rains, in plains, it's pains all claims.
As stains ingrain, your head now dangles low.

From shame, no birds can rise when life's unclaimed.
All wings so tame may cast off spells with task.
From knees, in faith we face what souls misplaced,
As pride removes the mask that task wouldn't ask.

The mask you wear is fear; it tells your tale.
When eyes so speak, your soul has started trail.

Ian A. Campbell

Your Turn

In hairpins, never lose your nerve.
All roads have curves; in bends, don't swerve.

On hills, it's skills beyond what's heard,
As gravity too, affect birds.

In race, you never mind their pace;
What's faced only sweat can brace.

In effort, work must start the chase,
But haste won't find success no place.

Where effort's true, all life so turns;
In things we earn, the jealous burns.

If eyes so seek and minds so churn,
As life so turns, be firm till urn.

Vice

In lives beset by storms, the winds don't cease.
In vice, none feels your breeze or knows its knocks.
In quiet, night's desires so takes your peace,
As waves and doubts don't stop on spinning rocks.

Where vice is nice, arrange to pay the price.
Those holding strong by faith avoid the crease.
As only lessons learnt from past suffice.
You'll only find your peace if spirit cease.

Your soul will gain its merit, standing judgment,
But neither friend nor cleric knows release.
Desires will fleece all good intentions meant.
As days now bent, not meant, so lays as please.

In lives beset by storms, the winds don't cease;
They'll howl while leaving feathers fold from itch.
Still cold the night-sweats find desire, the cheat.
With itch you twist not having mitts, you twitch.

Desires now having control, mind so fold.
You grieve and give reprieve where acts were lacks.
As minds no longer follows ways of old,
Your pride can't find the shame to change those facts.

In lives beset by storms, the winds won't cease
And neither friend nor cleric holds release.

Ian A. Campbell

The Mundane

A life mundane may take my flares,
As only promises lost compare,
When inner light no longer glares,
I fear a life that's caught in sneer.

A life mundane has taken flare.
Because I'm lost, who's right? What's clear?
Tomorrow's light, I want to share,
But inner light no longer glares.

As inner light no longer glares,
My soul, no longer plays as fair.
A life mundane so calms all fears.
But fears, now shared, shows what's clear.

A life mundane now claims my fears,
And only fight can see me clear.

LIFE AND RHYTHMS

The Lucky Few

A lucky few remains as whole in stew.
From heat all dreams evaporate by faith,
So hold your soul's essential pieces true.

When soul's essential pieces live in fear.
The ships without their compass move by waves,
And ones that're lost without their mast are clear.

The lucky few remain as whole in stew.
When pots become too hot, you skim the fat;
For souls will lose if life so chooses clues.

In storms, with ease, a life no longer please.
If blind, there're days in ways a life's unkind,
So souls must know degrees where efforts cease.

Those blue aren't few; you'll see who rues in stew.
Where winds so howl, the weak and hapless fall,
As fallen souls so wither, lives are blue.

When lost, no mast that's bare the winds shall lift,
And ones in treason sails off life's own cliffs.
From life, in life, when searching days of bliss,
With knuckles bare, you hold on through the mist.

Ian A. Campbell

In Dreams

All fools aspire to mountaintops
For greener views, forever distant,
But seldom reach to know the gaps.

A life unreal can find no path.
And ones that're true will find what's blue,
Yet both in life will hold their truth.

The real is grounded truth in shortcomings.
In lives that're false, all lies are cunning;
But life's the race, so watch the runnings.

A life unreal will live in dreams;
You merely sleep till days surrender,
As pages flow to night in reams.

In dreams, our minds are blind from lies,
We live obsessed, seeking pies;
While hoping fate so finds what hides.

The fool aspires to mountaintops,
Without the mind to see the gaps.
They overlook the rungs they've passed,
For views that'll claim a life in cost.

LIFE AND RHYTHMS

In Greed

When full, if wants still linger, know its greed,
As guilty hearts so seethe, the souls will feed.
They're turning wants to needs, while hungers plead,
As soul so feed you'll find unnamed creed.

If self-conceived, soul's desire's no need.
A craving stated, only minds can raise.
As conscience looks to plead, you'll see the seed.
In subtle ways, in haze we'll look for praise.

Between the fuss, the just must know the cusp.
If wishing's caught in thoughts for lives not bought,
The truth got sold as bait for gains in ups,
As dog devours dog, all souls are fraught.

The lost now chase their tails while draining souls.
As spirit starts to fold , all friends are cold,
Still looking glories dreamt but never cajoled;
They'll hold the anger, devils eyes foretold.

When full, if wants still linger, know it's greed.
Where wants so seethe, it's truth the soul must plead.

Ian A. Campbell

We Lie

We lie to lie—why?
And say to say—what?
Then live to live—how?

We fear to fear—whom?
And hide to hide—where?
Then lie to lie—why?

We run to run—where?
And see to see—what?
Then live to live—how?

We know to know—whom?
And ask to ask—what?
Then lie to lie—why?

You know to know— you
And live to live— now
Yet lie to lie—why?

Truth Depends

It's only when
You have a friend,
You may defend
The hurt words send;
At times even then
Your heart won't mend.

So let no friend
Try to defend
The hurt they send.
And then pretend
They're still your friend.

Should they pretend,
They're a vile friend
And that is when
You'll comprehend,
What time can't mend.

When they pretend,
The hurts they send,
Didn't affect friend;
Souls comprehend,
Lies make no friend.

Ian A. Campbell

It's only when
Words and deeds blend
Two hearts may bend
Toward life's zen,
Because that's when,
You'll know who's friend.

LIFE AND RHYTHMS

Right Expectations

In spinning winds, the devil grins.
Intention shows desire, as will
Exposes judgment's hidden sins,
But choice so tells how steep the hill.

Morality can hold no choice,
If greed defines what soul so needs.
As satisfaction carries price,
It's values held that stops what seeds.

All action dwells or hides in truth,
But one's potential lives in lies.
Where truth depends on life's uncouth,
What hides will always hold their whys.

When choice reveals what evil so wins,
You'll find the devil wearing grin.

Life and Rhythms

The City

I travel the marvel;
That's the empire state.
In faith on arrival,
Talent will mark the great.

Befittingly shitty,
A hell of a city.
Beautifully gritty,
Can be such a pity.

Broken hearts, shattered dreams.
In the jungle, they scream,
Trying to fit in seams,
As they search for its cream.

Befittingly witty,
Such a fucking city.
Attractively gritty,
So don't live in pity.

Talent will make the great
In the Empire State.

Ian A. Campbell

The Monte

Where morals shuffle, souls will make the split,
For greed's ahead of need, where price's too high.
In wrist, there's twist, no monte's short on wit,
We'll buy, those lies that wipe the cries from eyes.

The cries from lies, our souls too often buy,
In chance those lost forget a thief's intention.
The game's the lie, still fallen prey must die,
As gains alleged are loss to thieves' devotion.

By chance, with breeze and ease, the crowds will gather.
They'll scream as loud, so victim stays as proud.
With sleight of hand in shrouded clouds they flatter,
No matter chatter ego's the prey in crowds.

Where greed has trumped need, the price's too high,
In pride you'll pay the price as thieves so feed.
If minds deny what's true to bridge those lies,
The soul then holds in cause what's lost in creed.

In life's own dead-ends holding countless bends,
If hope is late it's lies that steal our spirit.
Where lies in self are felt the souls don't mend,
And gains without your works shall hold no merit.

LIFE AND RHYTHMS

Where greed's ahead of need, you're fighting ghost.
As monte's sleight of hands will need to flatter,
If morals shuffle, souls are playing host,
While letting devils claim what truly matter.

Ian A. Campbell

The Circus

In the circus, all lives are apart.
Where we're caught are in glories still sought.
And there're days you won't know your own heart.

Don't you fear the unknown, from that hell,
Where unending undead do so dwell,
It's to know there's no heaven in spell.

Should you claim or invite all that's hollow,
And so, settles by evading your truth,
It's to know, in your soul, you'll have sorrow.

In all things, we so fear what is near.
We're all fighting to claim our self-worth,
With a soul and a conscience that's clear.

It's from time we must steal what can stand.
Yet in things of this world that we borrow,
It's the soul that must change what's in hand.

In the circus, all lives are apart,
On those days when your spirit's so caught;
It's your mind you must pause when in fear,
So your conscience and soul can be clear.

LIFE AND RHYTHMS

The Unnecessary Walk

Unnecessary the walk that sparks the imagination.
But move with caution, holding flames to dream's liberation.

Where pavement makes connections, look in trees, and feel the breeze.
In passion's past, a life won't last if souls can't move from knees.

Relations tied to good libation hinders imagination.
No time to fight with things that break your synaptic connections.

Unnecessary the walk to known and named destinations,
Where footprints leave no marks, if holding strong to resignations.

As birds forget to fly, their walk will turn as necessary;
So souls can move from low, divorcing lies their minds now carry.

Unnecessary the walk that sparks the imagination,
Those dreams not past, once lost, now found still holds your liberation.

Ian A. Campbell

Your Dreams

Your dreams will only last so long.
And even those strong, will know their wrongs.

Internal wars will bear their scars;
No matter near or far, it's war.

The wars that're done yet never won
May leave a life to face those guns.

When life has stolen days from death,
It's joy that gives all life its breath.

The foolhardy is lost if asked.
They never plan their days in task.

Those living lives unaware shouldn't care,
Yet day or night, they live in fear.

Humility will come; don't run,
But hold your head as high in sun.

In glories, values taking rest,
Will leave all choices standing test.

LIFE AND RHYTHMS

The foolish live with hope in jest,
Refusing life and claiming blessed.

Your dreams will only last so long;
In wrongs those wise remain as strong.

Ian A. Campbell

Fiddler

I'm a fiddler, a man on a roof.
That's my truth, though the world must have proof.

On the journey, perceived a lush;
Destinations remain—so I push.

For my voyage, its surety…in self;
That may take all my talents from shelf.

But its poise that so signifies health,
And with practice my wealth will be felt.

We're all fiddlers that're sitting on roofs,
In our truths, may we'll find our own proofs.

Rhythms of Tomorrow

LIFE AND RHYTHMS

Time Is Limited

From darkness, life emerge to fill the cistern.
As times' commodity is self in worth,
Remember, life so comes as life returns.

From trees that bore our fruits, it's dust that follows.
The wheels are grinding, claiming lives in numbers.
Still, actions stand to serve your life's tomorrows.

From darkness, life emerges to fill all plains.
The plumes surrounding choice are one's own rains.
If erosions follows monsoons, souls have stains.

In being, time does hold our common rival.
As fate, tomorrow waits, no matter state;
All're tied together, fighting chance survival.

Your time has limits, death forever final.
Don't rest in days and get so caught in "oughts."
Tomorrow's truths will hold no other rival.

From darkness, life emerges to fill the cistern.
As one we came; as one, all life returns.
Commodity of time is life's lone value,
So live your life, while stealing joys from menu.

Ian A. Campbell

Time and Trade

Where time and trade have cast their shade,
Some made their means from dreaded scenes;
Where Abel, not having wage, has stayed,
As brother's slave, unseen in means.

Where time and trade so cast it's shade,
No soul atones where minds have caved.
Descents of Cain won't make the grade
As long as minds remain enslaved.

The game remains, all life so plays.
In trade, while wars are being raged;
The darkness claims some light in days,
As morals fight a mind that's caged.

As time and trade have cast their shade,
The human only stands by grade.
In minds, we trade, as souls are weighed.
The game remains, in life it's played.

As minds are looking shares in ecospheres,
Transforming worlds by earthly raids,
In droves the drones will leave this biosphere,
As time and trade so cast its shade.

LIFE AND RHYTHMS

As time and trade still cast it's shade,
Tomorrow's, wars are being waged.
As soul's internal lights are weighed,
The minds must fight what times have caged.

Ian A. Campbell

In Age

As verse not having meter hides its rhyme.
It's by the length of rope all fools so choke.
Those wise will summarize their goals in time,
For marching drums without its beats no joke.

In mind, the fool surmise what's true in time;
If times unkind they'll lose in rhythm their flow.
As time so flies, all values claimed, mine.
Where blind, those truths will hit all souls when low.

In age the fool may drown in shallow streams;
No roots yet planted, souls still haunted, wanting.
If rhyme's not fighting currents, watch the seams,
And know when irrigating doubt, it's daunting.

Those wise are counting; knowing times a mounting.
While fools are walking lonely roads a skylarking,
Their prose will leave no mark while days a counting,
As night approaches failure left a lurking.

Where verses loss their meters, leave the rhymes
And try abridging goals before it's time.

LIFE AND RHYTHMS

The Curve

If life tomorrow will,
And yesterday is found,
Today remains as still.

Don't look to life on hills;
They're stills that only work,
Can build by honing skills.

While living life there're scars.
Where fate does open gates,
It's fights that win those wars.

In truth, if faith does wane,
All path to victory stains;
But upwards curve remains.

As life tomorrow will,
If yesterday is found,
Today remains as still.

So celebrate the blips,
As past now flips to worlds
In days that're run by chips.

Ian A. Campbell

By talents, near and far
Our upward curves are bound,
To fights tomorrow's wars.

Because tomorrow will,
As yesterday is found,
Today the fight is still.

LIFE AND RHYTHMS

Times of Trouble

As time does tick, your pride must stay affixed.
If yesterday so brings tomorrows horrors,
Those values fighting night has morals fixed;
But pride that's false, upends secure tomorrows.

Morality is lost on downward slopes.
In times of trouble, virtues find their tricks.
As time outlasts all rope, you'll need to cope;
But know the troupes can't vote in virtue sticks.

Morality can't dwell where life has grays;
In black and white, your morals give no play.
In choice, as spirit originates ways,
The virtues, exercised in soul, may stay.

If yesterday had fears as trouble narrows,
As night so turns to day, where trouble follows,
What's false in pride upends secure tomorrows.

Ian A. Campbell

Clouds in Rainbow Skies

It's wrong to tell a lie while high.
In rainbow skies, the clouds are why
Tomorrow's crashes come from high,
In skies where lies so fly, oh my.

When high, you contemplate both sides,
As age now shows what life once hid.
In skies, the moments tease what glides,
As age so claims in shame what's slid.

For joys tomorrow, times at stake.
No one can escape fate, just wait.
The deeds in faith create those great,
And ones that're waiting, judgments late.

It's wrong to tell a lie while high,
Relish the highs; delay the whys,
Tomorrow's crash will tell the why.
As clouds so move in rainbow skies.

LIFE AND RHYTHMS

Today's Troubles

When the mind's in dismay, what will play?
If your heart is too kind, then who's blind?
In the fray, it's your heart that may sway.

When your emotions are fraught, for what sought?
They're a part of the fights to be fought.
You must look to those thoughts for what's caught.

In all wishes, it's values that fish,
If there're choices then morals in dish,
Still we follow those blind on a wish.

As intentions predict none in pain,
It's so plain; all are met by some rains,
And those even in fanes have their stains.

For the souls, it's through faith we maintain,
It's the house that protects us in rains,
And where false, all our works are in vain.

As the troubles we're facing may stay,
When the mind's in dismay, who has sway?
It's your mind that must find what's in play.
In the fray, it's your hearts that may sway.

About the Author

Ian A. Campbell immigrated to the United States from Jamaica W.I. in 1985. An avid student, he received his bachelor's degree in sociology from Binghamton University and his master's in real estate development from New York University.

Campbell is a poet whose writings have encapsulate the human experience with a philosophical bent. He's in search of meaning in each individual life as we search for rightness and purpose. His greatest hope is to produce works that can make a difference and become works that truly matters.

His first collection, *Life and Livity* is an emotional journey with powerful life lessons. In this work, the introspective Campbell tries to place a firm grasp on life and all its complexities. They are a critical look at our current society and pushes the envelope to where we may go in the future.

www.ingramcontent.com/pod-product-compliance
Lightning Source LLC
Chambersburg PA
CBHW021440080526
44588CB00009B/623